ZANY NIAGARA

The Funny Things People Say About Niagara Falls

by Paul Gromosiak

Illustrations by John Hardiman

Introduction by Brian Meyer

First printing June 1992
Cover Design by John Hardiman
Printed by Artcraft Burow Printers

To my brother, Michael Richard Gromosiak

In eighteenth century England, newspaper accounts of conditions in North America were often exaggerated. For example, absolutely incredible fish stories were told to a gullible public. While staying in London, the great American satirist and statesman, Benjamin Franklin, decided to have fun with the Europeans, so he wrote the following report, which is the subject for this book's cover.

"The inhabitants of Canada are making preparations for a Cod and Whale Fishery this summer in the Upper Lakes. Ignorant People may object that the Upper Lakes are fresh, and that Cod and Whale are Salt-water Fish: But let them know, Sir, that Cod, like other Fish, when attacked by their Enemies, fly into any Water where they think they can be safest; that Whales, when they have a mind to eat Cod, pursue them wherever they fly; and that the grand Leap of the Whale in that Chase up the Fall of Niagara is esteemed by all who have seen it, as one of the finest Spectacles in Nature."*

Niagara Falls, Icon of the American Sublime, by Elizabeth McKinsey, Cambridge University Press, New York, 1985, p. 27.

iv

Acknowledgements

This book could not have been written without the able assistance of John Hardiman, whose talents transformed my crude sketches into works of art. I met with visitors by the Falls with the permission of Mario Pirastru, whose kindness and understanding will be forever appreciated. Much of my inspiration came from the staff of the Schoellkopf Geological Museum, and I cannot say enough about them as educators and friends. I am also indebted to Donald E. Loker for his patient and generous assistance.

Paul Gromosiak

Introduction

by Brian Meyer

It was a muggy August night and darkness had fallen on Niagara Falls.

A college buddy from New York City gazed at the glorious cascade of water, now showcased by a brilliant burst of man-made light. He stared at the falls, then cast his eyes skyward to the full moon. It looked like yet another splendid prop in this fabulous show.

"I understand how they light up the falls," said this college junior. "But how do they get the spotlight to shine on the moon?" he asked in utter seriousness.

When highly-respected Niagara Falls historian Paul Gromosiak approached me with the idea of publishing a breezy tome on the funny things people say about this tourist attraction, the scene of my college chum gazing at the moon immediately popped into my mind. Paul didn't have to do much to sell his idea. I loved it.

Even as a kid, I sensed the falls exuded a zany quality. With its outlandish names like Goat Island, Devil's Hole and Cave of the Winds, it wasn't difficult for a kid with an over-active imagination to ponder some crazy thoughts. Like if he risked coming in contact with Satan in the Devil's Hole locale and what type of food he should stash in his pockets for all the goats he might encounter while touring their namesake island (little did he know that the last goats to occupy the island died in the late 1700's!)

As a student, I remember learning about how President William McKinley visited the Falls on the very day of his assassination. Only hours before he was gunned down at the Pan-American Exposition in Buffalo, McKinley had marvelled at nature's majesty on Goat Island and Luna Island.

As a young adult, I saw the Hitchcock-style thriller *Niagara*, in which Marilyn Monroe played a faithless wife scheming to kill her husband while on their honeymoon. This 1952 flick used Niagara Falls as a magnificent backdrop. I couldn't help but wonder how many spouses had knocked-off their lovers while regaling in what local P.T. Barnums have long billed as the Honeymoon Capitol of the World.

Several years ago, when Paul Gromosiak approached my company about publishing his first two fine works, our association soon turned into a crash course on fascinating falls facts. Perhaps the most intriguing discovery I made while editing Paul's two books was a phenomenon called the Dividing of the Waters.

I was truly amazed to learn that there is actually a spot at the head of Goat Island where the river divides into what we call the Canadian and American rapids. I stared in disbelief one lovely spring day as Paul tossed a twig into the waters to show me the calm where the river divides. How weird, I thought. How zany.

And now we come to the third book in what will hopefully be a long series of Gromosiak volumes on Niagara Falls. You, dear reader, are about to embark on a zany literary tour. You'll learn about visitors who actually thought there was an underwater restaurant beneath the falls, about a woman who wondered aloud if a barrel lying in the rapids contained the body of Jimmie Hoffa and about some folks back in the late 1800s who believed the falls were turned off every Wednesday.

A word of caution. By its very definition, *Zany Niagara* is offbeat. It's not written for the stuffy, scholarly-types. And it's penned in a breezy, anecdote-driven style that invites readers to browse through its chapters, selecting those subjects that most interest them.

When you finally make it to the end of this book, you'll note that Paul has included an Appendix. It's a blank page for readers to jot down their own recollections of zany utterances about Niagara Falls.

We encourage you to pencil-in your own contributions to this slim, humor-laden volume. And we thank you in advance for joining us on what we hope will be a most enjoyable — and unusual — armchair tour that focuses on the zany side of Niagara Falls!

Brian Meyer
1992

Foreword

Many people, indeed, ask and say zany things about Niagara Falls. The awesome spectacle often seems to cause a loss for words and relaxes a few inhibitions. This book relates actual words of the famous and the not-so-famous. Some names are not given in order to protect the guilty.

"Always laugh when you can — it is cheap medicine. Mirthfulness is a philosophy not well understood. It is the sunny side of existence."

Niagara Falls Gazette Weekly
November 7, 1855

"Thoughts on Visiting Niagara"

I wonder how long you've been a roarin'
    At this infernal rate;
I wonder if all you've been a porin'
    Could be ciphered on a slate.

I wonder how such a thund'rin' sounded
    When all New York was woods;
I suppose some Indians have been drownded
    When rains have raised your floods.

I wonder if wild stags and buffaloes
    Hav'nt stood where now I stand;
Well, 'spose — bein'; scared at first — they stub'd
their toes,
    I wonder where they'd land!

I wonder if the rainbow's been a shinin'
    Since sunrise at creation;
And this water-fall been underminin'
    With constant spateration!

That Moses never mentioned ye, I've wondered,
    While other things describin'
My conscience! How loud you must have thunder'd
    While the deluge was subsidin'!

My thoughts are strange, magnificent and deep,
    While I look down on thee.
Oh! What a splendid place for washing sheep
    Niagara would be!
And oh! What a tremendous water power
    Is wasted o'er its edge!
One man might furnish all the world with flour
    With a single privilege.

I wonder how many times the lakes have all
    Been emptied over here?
Why Clinton did't feed the Grand Canal
    From hence, I think is queer."

Anonymous

Do Fish Climb Up the Falls?

There are no animals or plants near the falls that can't be found elsewhere in the Great Lakes region. The Niagara River, its falls, and the surrounding fertile lands are immersed in an ever changing climate which luxuriantly affects the growth and behavior of life forms. The human audience often reacts to this unusual natural theater either innocently or with exaggeration.

During most of its history, the Niagara River has had an abundance of fish and about the same number of related stories. For example, in 1710, a group of Native Americans visiting Europe told their hosts that there were so many fish going over the falls that they formed a heap in the lower river of an infinite number of dead or dying fish easily picked out of the water by hand!

In 1721, a French Canadian, named Borossow, claimed he had seen someone catch an 86 pound trout somewhere in Niagara country. He also said a priest told him he had seen two men carrying a pike that measured at least six feet long.

A monsieur Bonnefons, a visitor from France in 1753, said the dead fish in the lower Niagara River did *not* go over the falls, because had they done so, they would have disappeared below the falls. He claimed the fish died in their valiant attempts to go *up* the falls.

When Mark Twain wrote about his visit to Niagara Falls in 1869, his observations definitely contradicted those of the Native Americans in 1710. In fact, his comments contradicted those of many other people. Twain said, "the opportunities for fishing are not surpassed in the country; in fact they are not even equalled elsewhere. Because, in other localities, certain places in the streams are much better than others; but at

Niagara one place is just as good as another, for the reason that the fish do not bite anywhere, and so there is no use in your walking five miles to fish, when you can depend on being just as unsuccessful nearer home. The advantages of this state of things have never heretofore been properly placed before the public."

There's something fishy about Twain's account. Why, when he stood by the river's shore, all he had to do was bend over and pull a fish out of the water with his bare hands. Yes. That's how may fish there were in the water.

In July of 1884, the *Niagara Falls Gazette* reported the following whale of a tale.

"A Big Fish"

"The rumor that a big fish had been caught at La Salle Friday afternoon created quite a sensation on the street. Had it not grown so rapidly in size and reached such enormous dimensions perhaps a few might have believed the story. As it was we believe two or three took the 2:16 train to view the monster which was variously estimated at from two to four feet in length. That the Niagara between this place and Tonawanda — whether La Salle or some other place is not known — is the abode of a sea serpent is believed by not a few. Some time ago a Tonawanda paper contained a lengthy description of the monster as furnished by an eyewitness. Tonawanda, now that the temperance camp has been abandoned, may be able to support a sea serpent. It may even get as far down the river as La Salle, but we doubt if it will ever be seen below that point, surely not on our fishing grounds."

In 1911, a mysterious note appeared on a postcard sent from Niagara Falls. "Wait till you see the picture of my fish. Lots of water here but no fishing."

People are still very interested Niagara's fish. They have been asking questions such as:

"Do you have ladders for the salmon to come up the falls?"

"How many fish go over the falls each day?"

"Do fish climb up the falls?"

"What's the fine for going in the water after a carp?"

Years ago, great numbers of birds often died at the falls, causing wild speculations as to the cause. In 1783, monsieur Bonnefons wrote that:

> "birds which fly over the fall are drawn into it in spite of themselves, by the force of the air. I am not so sure of this fact, which, however, is not lacking in probability, since there is often seen there a rainbow which seems strongly to attract the birds who direct their flight into it, where they become confused and drenched, lacking strength to ascend. And it may perhaps be only birds of passage, for those which inhabit the neighborhood are so accustomed to the rainbow and to the noise of the fall that they know how to preserve themselves, since they are seldom seen there, although there are a great many of them in this vicinity."

Many other early visitors to Niagara thought they saw the same phenomenon, but there is no proof that birds die in that manner. It is now thought that the water-fowl, the usual victims, died going over at night when the falls were enveloped in fog.

The most obvious of the resident birds by the falls is the Ring-billed Gull. It has enjoyed a tremendous increase in its population this century. Its competitive and seemingly playful nature has made it attractive to those local citizens and visitors who delight in watching its feeding frenzies. Listen to its vocalizations, watch it soar over the falls, and it is possible to become mesmerized.

> "Suddenly the skies filled with gulls, soaring in circles, in a frenzy, as if searching for something lost. Then, as if one of them had shouted 'last one out of here is an eagle's uncle,' they instantly dispersed."
>
> Paul Gromosiak

The red-winged blackbird nests on the shores of the islands above the falls, and the male is extremely protective of his nestlings and mate. One time, while crossing the bridge to Luna Island, a young man was struck repeatedly on the head by a very angry blackbird. In desperation, the terrified man went down on his hands and knees and crawled, like a baby, to the small island. Quite embarassed, his only comment to onlookers was, "that bird was really mad."

Some zany questions recently asked by visitors about Niagara's birds are:

"Does the red-winged blackbird come in any other colors?"

"How many birds do you get here?"

"Did you know there's a duck in the water?"

"Where are all the male mallards?"

Believe it or not, some people have actually thrown animals into the rapids above the falls. Now for the good news. A few of them survived their trips over the falls! The following account appeared in the *Niagara Falls Gazette,* Wednesday, November 16, 1887.

"A hound owned by H. C. Fuchs and thrown into the rapids, and was seen to go over the falls eighteen months ago, made its second appearance on earth last week Wednesday. He was located on Main Street, but declined to acknowledge any acquaintance with his former master."

Once a young couple watched a chipmunk scurry under a railing toward the rapids. Not able to see where the creature ended up, the young man looked at his companion and remarked, "I hope he didn't jump in."

The lands around the American side of the falls now have a substantial black squirrel population. The little critters are often fed and photographed by tourists who ask questions such as:

"How did the black squirrels get here?"

"Why are there more black squirrels than gray squirrels on Goat Island?"

After his parents encouraged him not to be shy, a little boy went up to the Falls Historian and asked, "are there any frogs by the falls?" The Historian answered, "there aren't any frogs by the falls. Why? Look at the rapids. Could a tadpole survive there? Of course, not!"

All during the summer of 1987, a very large tree trunk projected horizontally about twenty feet from the center of the brink of the American Fall, its few remaining roots securely lodged in the rocks. People were, naturally, quite interested in the unusual sight. They asked questions such as:

"How long has that tree been there?"

"When will the tree go over?"

"How did that tree get there?"

"Why doesn't someone remove that log?"

"What keeps that log there?"

Why Doesn't the Gorge Fill Up?

Many people wonder why the Great Lakes don't become empty after all their waters pour over Niagara Falls. They must have forgotten about Nature's wonderful "hydrologic cycle," her means of travelling all over the world, watering her plants along the way. Oh yes, it's true that parts of the falls have been dry or frozen for short periods of time, but since the end of the last ice age, about twelve thousand years ago, water has been flowing into the great Niagara River uninterrupted from Lake Erie.

Even some famous people have wondered about the source of Niagara's water. According to *The Humorous Mr. Lincoln*, by Keith W. Jennison, in the autumn of 1848, long before he had become famous, Abraham Lincoln visited Niagara Falls. He is reported to have said, "the thing that struck me most forcibly was, where in the world did all that water come from?"

Of course, people also often ask questions such as: "are there ever floods by the falls, or why doesn't the gorge fill up?" Even the purported discoverer of the falls, Father Louis Hennepin, couldn't understand where all the water went after going over the falls. He said, in 1678, "I could not conceive how it came to pass, that four great Lakes, the least of which is 400 Leagues [about 1,200 miles or 1,931 kilometers] in compass, should empty themselves one into another, and then all centre and discharge themselves at this Great Fall, and yet not drown a good part of America."

At Niagara, waterfalls and rockfalls go hand in hand, side by side, or alone. Fortunately, most of the time, people are not killed or injured when the rocks decide to move. There is a humorous story of a close encounter with the fall of a large piece of Table Rock, a ledge that once projected far out into the top of the gorge by the Horseshoe Fall. Sometime in the 1850's, according to the *Niagara Falls Gazette* of September 12, 1860, a presumably young couple had a truly earth-shaking experience. The young man narrates the details.

"In the years which have elapsed since I first visited Niagara, I find many changes have been made. The precipice has visibly receded, and the voracious torrent still keeps eating into the river's rocky bed from year to year. Table Rock has fallen, but that was partly caused by me; the Tower (Terrapin Tower, a stone tower once located at the brink of the Horse-shoe Fall) is still more perilously towards the edge, and momentoes of new victims are erected here and there along the river's bank. The same shopkeepers with their goods; and the same loitering couples, still under 20 years of age, and looking as if ten years was nothing to them, restored the old panorama step by step. The effect was magical and having again got in good prac-tice of handing out quarters. I was several times on the point of feeling about me to see if I had not ten years or so to spare along with the rest.

I said I had something to do with the falling of Table Rock, that broad shelf on the Canada side which in 1850 jutted over the very cauldron of the seething water, but which tumbled into it on a certain day in the month of June of that, by me, well remembered year. About noon on that day I accompanied a lady from the Clifton house (a hotel located on the site of the present day Oakes Garden Theatre, Niagara Falls, Canada) to the falls. Arriving at Table Rock we left our carriage, and as we approached the projecting platform I pointed out to my companion a vast fissure or crack which traversed the entire base of the rock, remarking that it looked wider than it had ever appeared to me before. The lady almost shuddered as she looked at it, and shrinking back, declared that she did not care about going to edge. 'Ah,' said I taking her hand, 'you might as well come on now that you are here I hardly think that the rock will take a notion to fall merely because we are on it.'

The platform jutted from the mainland some sixty feet, but to give the visitor a still more fearful projection over the raging waters, a wooden bridge or staging had been thrust beyond the extreme edge for some ten feet. This terminated in a small box for visitors to stand on, and was kept in its position and enabled to bear weight by a ponderous load of stones heaped upon its inner end. The day was very bright and hot, and it being about lunch time at the hotel, but few visitors were out as we occupied the dizzy perch alone. We gazed fearfully upon the awful scene, we stretched our heads timidly over the frightful depth below, and we felt our natures quelled in every fibre by the deafening roar that seemed to saturate us as it were with an undefinable dread. 'This is a terrible place,' said I. 'Look under there and see on what a mere shell we stand. For years and years, the tooth of the torrent, in that jetting angry stream has been gnawing out that hollow, and some day this place must fall.' My companion shuddered, and drew herself together in fear. Our eyes swept the roaring circle of the waters once again; we gazed about in tearful fascination, when suddenly turning our looks upon one another, each recognized a corresponding fear. 'I do not like this place,' exclaimed I quickly. 'The whole base of this rock is probably disintegrated, and perhaps sits poised in a succession of steps or notches, ready to fall out and topple down at any unusual perturbation. That fissure there seems to me to be more than usually wide today! I think we had better leave, for I do not fancy such a finish, and besides, my paper *must* be published next week.'

With these very words, the latter uttered half jocosely, though not without alarm, I seized my companion's hand, and, in absolute panic, we fled as fast as our feet could carry us toward what might be called the shore. We burst into a laugh when we regained the land, and jumping into our carriage, felt actually as if we had made a fortunate escape. We rolled back toward Clifton, but before we had proceeded two minutes on our way, a thundering report, like the explosion of an earthquake, burst upon us with a long roar; the ground trembled beneath our wheels. We turned to find Table Rock had fallen. We were the last upon it, and it was doubltless the unusual perturbation caused by our flying footsteps that disturbed the exactness of its equilibrium, and thrilled it from its final poise.

In a minute more, the road was filled with hurrying people, and during the following half hour we were told a hundred times in advance of the next morning's journals that a lady and gentleman who were on Table Rock had gone down the falls. We are told that the trot of a dog would shake old London Bridge from end to end, when it would not be disturbed by the rolling of heavily loaded trains. Table Rock had probably not been run upon in that way I have described for years — perhaps never; and therefore, whenever I hear it spoken of, I always shudder and feel as if I had something to do with its fall."

Can this story be believed? Can a tale be taller? Who knows, though? No mention was made of the size of either the lady or the gentleman.

Unfortunately, or fortunately, whatever the case may be, many people gamble, a habit that has been around as long as

Homo sapiens has walked the earth. At Niagara, bets were usually placed on the fate of a daredevil, starting with Sam Patch, the first person to challenge the river. Oh, yes. People do bet about other things at Niagara, such as the speed of the rapids, the heights of the falls, and so on. In 1990, people were placing bets as to when the large red drum at the brink of the American Fall would roll over.

In the *Niagara Falls Gazette Weekly* of October 31, 1855, there appeared an article about a man who bet he could prove that "this side of the Niagara River was the other side." Well, someone bet him ten dollars that he was wrong. Accepting the challenge, the man pointed to the opposite side of the river and asked:

"Is not that one side of the river?"
"Yes," was the answer.
Agreed, said the man; "and is not this the other side?"
"Yes," said the other.
"Then," said the man, "pay me my ten dollars, for, by your own confession, I have proved that this side of the river is the other side."

The ugly foam in the lower river below the falls is composed mostly of natural materials, despite its artificial appearance. Canadian scientists have carefully analyzed it recently to determine its exact composition, primarily decaying algae. All that work was not necessary or correct, a local woman said in March of 1990. Her four-year-old son bet he knew how the foam got there and of what it was made. "It came from the gulls," he said.

Just about every winter, masses of ice come down from Lake Erie and accumulate in the gorge just below the falls, often becoming a solid mass from shore to shore, an "ice bridge." The following romantic announcement of the formation of such a structure appeared in the *Niagara Gazette* on Wednesday, January 18, 1888.

"Marriage Extraordinary"

"A correspondent sends us the following: 'On the night of January 13th, Miss Canada West, of Ontario, was united to New York, Esq., of the Empire State. Nuptials performed by the venerable Jack Frost, Vicar of the Cave of the Winds. The great Falls thundered their congratulations and the Whirlpool Rapids echoed and reechoed the song.'"

In March of that same year, a man was quoted in the *Niagara Falls Gazette*, expressing his disappointment with that winter's ice bridge.

"Gawl durn it," said he, "I never was so sold in my life, swan to man if I ever see sech a swindle. When they talked about an ice bridge I s'posed it *wuz* a bridge, reaching from bank to bank, made up o'spray and sich, so's to you could walk under it as well as over it. Well, sir, me'n my wife went down there and by gum't wan't nothin' but an old ice jam sech as we have all winter long in the creek down to hum. Jest a plain sheet o' scrap ice stretchin' an' nothin' more. It's a blame fraud; that's all it is."

During the latter part of the last century, daring entrepreneurs would erect shabby shanties on the ice bridge close to the Canadian-United States border. They sold, among other things, intoxicating beverages to the thirsty crowds. The lucrative trade was not favored by the authorities, but arrest was difficult. For example, as an American law officer approached, the shanty could easily be moved closer to or over the border. "Sorry, officer, but I'm not in your jurisdiction," must have been said innumerable times.

Unfortunately, many years ago, it was the custom at Niagara to take advantage of visitors, so as to profit financially. Misdeeds were committed and lies were told freely. Shame! Shame! Shame! But...sometimes a few people deserved to be mistreated. Such was the following case of poetic justice reported in the *Daily Cataract Journal* on February 22, 1901.

"And Charlie Believed It"

"Being the Tale of How Conductor Green Explained the Formation of Niagara's Ice Bridge to a Gullible Young Man"

"He was a well dressed young man, who felt the responsiblity of acting as escort for two women, and he was as talkative as the average $8-a-week clerk placed in the same position. His brilliant displays of wit, often at the expense of his fellow passengers, served to keep his two companions convulsed with merriment. They were on their way to Niagara Falls on one of the Lehigh Valley's branch trains, and genial Jim Green was punching tickets and serving at the same time as a target for the young man's witty sarcasms. Jim bore the lively teasing of the clerk with the (patience) of a Tonawanda reservation Native American, and, like the noble red man, waited for his revenge. The opportunity came.

'They say the ice bridge is fine now,' remarked one of the young women, reflecting on her destination. 'Isn't it wonderful how that great bridge is formed? Do you know, Charlie, what causes the water to freeze in such a strange way? You seem to know everything.'

The young man smiled, complacently. His companion's questionable compliment tickled him, but for once he was without a ready answer.

'I'm sure I never gave the matter a thought,' he said hesitatingly. 'Just wait, I'll ask the conductor. I say, Mr. Green, would you be so kind as to inform us under what peculiar atmospheric conditions the beautiful icy highway below the falls is formed. We're quite undecided how it assumes its wonderfully majestic appearance.'

'That's easy,' replied Green, swinging his punch on his little finger and speaking in all seriousness. 'You see, conditions have to be right to start with. It must be a bright, sunny day and very cold. You know when the sun is shining the reflection upon the spray rising below the falls forms a huge rainbow, entirely spanning the gorge. If it's cold enough, the spray freezes, forming a coating over the rainbow, and thus the bridge is started, much as engineers first swing a single cable across a river when a bridge is to be erected. Continued adhesion of the spray to the bow with constant freezing weather finishes the bridge. I tell you, Mother Nature has given us our best lessons in civil engineering.'

'That's so,' said the young man. 'Isn't it wonderful? I'm sure I'd never have thought of that, and we're much obliged to you.'

Conductor Green's face was as expressionless as the tickets he was taking as he moved down the aisle, but one of the young women was heard by the passenger behind them to remark: 'Truly, Bell, I think Charley believes it.'

The ice bridge sometimes reminds people of a glacier, and, in fact, it sometimes behaves like a glacier. Its tremendous power pushed the Falls View Bridge, now commonly known as the Honeymoon Bridge, right off its foundations in January of 1938. The following story about the supposed explosion of a glacier at Niagara Falls probably was manufactured by someone who fell and suffered a head injury while walking on the perilous surface of an ice bridge. According to the *Niagara Falls Gazette* of Wednesday, February 6, 1867, the story first appear in the London *Engineer* and was apparently believed by many people all over Europe. The *Gazette* suggested that local businessmen take advantage of the story and use it for "replenishing their exchequers."

"A Wonderful Story about the Explosion of a Glacier at Niagara Falls"

"Not far from the Falls of Niagara was a glacier, belonging to a company which realized enormous profits by the sale of the ice in the western cities during the summer months. One day, an aurora borealis of magnificent proportions was observed wheeling its shafts several nights in succession in the northern sky, causing two lightning conductors on the top of the glacier to emit a long electrical flame of a boiling bluish color. In the meantime, a boiling noise was heard inside the glacier, accompanied with a disengagement of gas and occasional loud detonations. A captain of the militia ventured to enter an opening in the ice with light, when the glacier burst with an explosion that shook the whole country. Happily, nobody was killed except the unfortunate captain, of whom not a trace could be found. The glacier contained 16,000 tons of ice, and after the explosion there was a fall of luke-warm water over a space of 500 yards in diameter. The theory of the cause of the explosion was that the two lightning conductors on the glacier acted under the influence of the electricity as the two poles of a voltaic battery, and decomposed the ice into a mixture of oxygen and hydrogen gases, which of course exploded with resistless power on the introduction of a light."

Isn't It Alright to Jump?

The Niagara Falls, and the rapids above and below them, have drawn many people who have desired fame, fortune, excitement, a serious challenge, or a quick end to their problems. For whatever reasons, the acts these people commit, though really of a serious nature, are often perceived as humorous either by themselves or onlookers.

The first Niagara daredevil was Sam Patch, who more than once dove into the lower river from a ladder about 100 feet high, erected near the site of the now famous Cave of the Winds walk. The following poem appeared in the album of a local hotel a few years after Patch's stunts of 1829.

> "These are the great Niagara Falls,
> Down which Sam Patch did jump;
> The people said he'd break his neck—
> He only hurt his rump."
>
> Anonymous

During the past two centuries, some people have either not followed through with their plans or falsely claimed to have successfully performed stunts by the falls or in the river. Therefore, advertisements by daredevils or their managers were not always taken seriously by the editors of the local newspapers. The following article appeared in the *Niagara Falls Gazette* on Wednesday, September 11, 1889.

"Brodie Blows"

"Early Saturday morning it was currently reported on the streets the 'Steve' Brodie, another daring-feat crank, had plunged over the Horseshoe Falls, dressed in a rubber suit. A *Gazette* representative hearing of Brodie being at Niagara Falls, Ont., immediately hied himself hither and succeeded in locating the personage at the Waverly House at that place. 'Press always welcome,' declared the hero(?) who was reclining on a bed making wry faces over pain in his back. The story of the occurrence, as told by the party, is as follows: Brodie; Ernest Gerold, of the New York *Sun;* John McCarthy, *World;* W. E. Harding, *Police Gazette,* and John Ledger, a New York life-saver, arrived at Suspension Bridge (now a part of the City of Niagara Falls, New York) Friday afternoon and proceeded to Niagara Falls, Ont., where they registered under assumed names, to escape police interference. About 4 A.M. the party left the hotel and were driven to a point two hundred feet above the Falls. Brodie stripped, padded himself with cotton-batten, and entered his man-shaped rubber-arrangement, which was then inflated. Before going far, he lost a paddle which he had carried to guide his course. A moment after he reached the brink and plunged into the boiling cauldron of rushing water. Two minutes elapsed before he was seen, when he appeared at the surface and the life-saver swam out to him and secured a rope around his body. Brodie, when taken out, was rubbed and bathed with brandy. Blood oozed from his mouth, nose, and ears. He was taken back to the hotel, where he was examined by a local physician, who failed to find anything the matter with him. Brodie said that he must either go over Niagara Falls or to an insane asylum, as it was constantly on his mind, and had got to be a mania. Brodie said, 'a man is a fool to go over Niagara Falls.' When asked if he would go over again he said, 'that unless someone would pay $1,000 he would never attempt it again.' This reads more like a gilt-edged romance than a truthful statement, and probably after time... it will be made public that the affair was the result of an imaginative brain. One fact which goes to disprove the story is that of Ledger's swimming out in the turbulent waters so near the Falls and securing the floater. It is said by everyone, who has viewed the place referred to, that it is impossible for a human being to live in such waters.

Saturday afternoon as Brodie was about to take the train for New York City, he was arrested by Chief McDougall, of the Ontario Police, on the charge of attempting suicide by going over Niagara Falls.

Brodie in answer to the charge said that he did not attempt suicide, but did it to show the world that the trip could be made, and to illustrate the usefulness of a rubber suit for life-saving purposes.

The police magistrate told him he did not believe he went over the Falls at all, and the whole thing was gotten up by himself and friends to humbug the people, and if he did not go over the Falls to say so and he would discharge him, or if he persisted in saying he went over, he would go with the case against him of attempted suicide, and told him there was a penalty in the Dominion covering such things.

Brodie said: 'If I tell you I did not go over will you let me go?'

'Yes.'

'Well, then, I did not go over, and I am off.'

The Magistrate: 'Hold on, I am not through with you yet.' Here he wrote the following declaration and asked Brodie to sign it:

'I, Stephen Brodie, the party we then charged

hereby declare that I did not go over Niagara Falls as within charged, and that the story of having gone over was all for the purpose of a speculation and untrue.'

Brodie asked the police magistrate if that was an oath. The police magistrate answered him in the affirmative. Brodie then replied: 'I cannot perjure myself. I am a Catholic and cannot sign that.'

The magistrate then began the examination. Alexander Fraser, barrister, acted as counsel for Brodie, Chief-of-Police McDougall and George Phemister, agent Canadian Associated Press, testified that Brodie did not complain any of being shaken up. Thomas Emory, hackman, who drove the party from the Falls to the Waverly House, and others, testified as to the stories they had heard of the exploit.'

After the police magistrate summed up the evidence, he bound the prisoner over in $500 bonds on his own recognizance to keep the laws of the Dominion, especially that of not attempting going over the Falls for one year. After the prisoner had signed the document he immediately left for the American side.

His Friends, Harding, Jerold, and McCarthy, as soon as they heard Brodie was arrested, made themselves scarce, no doubt fearing arrest for aiding and abetting an attempted suicide.

That much for one side of the story, but the other side needs a little looking into, which upon being done, shows it to be a fake of even worse kind than Graham's. (Graham was a man who said he would go over the falls in a barrel, but never showed up the day he was supposed to do it.) About 9 o'clock Friday night John Ross, an engineer of the 'Maid of the Mist,' who sleeps in company with the fireman on board the steamer, had occasion to go up the bank. When partly up he met four men carrying bundles, one of which was round, apparently the pantaloons of the rubber outfit. Not noticing anything particular he walked on, but turned around soon after to find that they had disappeared in the bushes. In the morning John Lally, the fireman, noticed a hack coming down the road containing four men, who made for the bushes near the wharf. He called the engineer and they both watched the proceedings. About 15 minutes later the three emerged carrying something that looked like a man, and put it into the hack. The rig was hurried away, and Brodie's feat was accomplished. The engineer recognized the party as the ones he had seen the night before, and says he is positive that that was as near going over the Falls as Brodie went."

Some of Niagara's daredevils did things that were not very daring. The *Niagara Falls Gazette Weekly* of August 27, 1856, satirized a "stunt" which took place just below the falls. The article mentions a Lunar Bow, a faint rainbow, often a complete circle, formed in the mist of the American Fall on moonlit nights.

"An Unparalleled Performance"

"The engagement was made some days previous to last Friday that a Mr. Jackson, of this place, would on that day undertake to swim across the Niagara from a point between the Biddle Stairs (a wooden staircase into the gorge on Goat Island, used from 1829 to 1925) and the Horseshoe Fall. Well, Friday came, usually as it does, Jackson was on hand as per promise, and a few people collected to witness the feat. Jackson entered a boat which was manned with two or three young men and a clothes line. Jackson was taken to the proposed starting place and took to the water 'like a thing of life.' The boat took the lead, and when well into the current the aforesaid line was quickly dropped astern, after which Jackson was enabled to keep within a few feet of the boat until near the opposite side below the ferry landing, when he cut loose and gained the shore. His return we are happy to announce, was safe, for no accident ever befell a ferry boat at this point.

We believe this is the first feat of the kind ever performed here. The strangers witnessing the performance ought to have taken measures to present this man with a leather medal.

A gentleman of this village, determined not to be outdone, requests us to announce that he will undertake to climb the Lunar Bow, on an occasion to be announced the the proper quarter, and that there will be no postponement on account of the weather."

The most famous and prosperous of all the Niagara daredevils was the one and only Jean Francois Gravelet, better known by his stage name, Blondin. In the summer of 1859, he became the first tight-rope walker to perform over the dangerous gorge below the falls. Before he was about to begin his first performance, he was interviewed by the local press. When asked about his feelings about a possible accident, he good-naturedly responded, "There be one American Fall, and one Canada Fall; when Blondin falls, there will be one French fall."

The first person to ride a barrel over the Horseshoe Fall (no one performs stunts at the American Fall because of the numerous rocks below) was a middle-aged lady, Anna Edson Taylor, affectionately known as "Annie." After one postponement, she ended up making the plunge on her 46th birthday. What a brave woman! Wait a minute! When asked if she would make the trip again her response was, "If it was with my dying breath, I would caution anyone against attempting the feat. I will never go over the falls again. I would sooner walk up to the mouth of a cannon knowing it was going to blow me to pieces than make another trip over the falls."

George Stathakis, the fifth person to go over the Horseshoe Fall in a barrel, successfully made the plunge on July 5, 1930, but he suffocated after his craft was held under water below the Horseshoe for about 22 hours. His pet turtle, "Sonny Boy," survived the trip. Stathakis had said, just before his stunt, "if I die, the turtle will carry the secret of the trip and reveal it at the proper time." Well, according to Andy O'Brian, author of *Daredevils of Niagara*, the turtle "never said a thing."

The seventh person to go over the Horseshoe Fall, William A. Fitzgerald, alias Nathan T. Boya, had better luck than poor Mr. Stathakis. William, the only Black American to perform the dangerous stunt, didn't want publicity and seriously sought anonymity. When asked if he were an IBM employee, which he was, he replied, "an IBM employee would not engage in this sort of thing (going over the falls in a "barrel") from what I understand, they wear white shirts."

On June 5, 1990, a young man from Tennessee went over the Horseshoe Fall in a kayak, quite convinced he would survive. He didn't. His death left many questions left unanswered. Local officials were interviewed by all the media. One reporter's question stood out from all the rest. "Why didn't he (the kayaker) go over the American Falls? He was an American citizen, wasn't he?"

Through the years, the following comments have been made by visitors to the falls. They joked about all types of dangerous behavior from wading in the river to riding in a barrel over one of the falls.

"Isn't it alright to jump?"

"What would they fine me for taking a bath in the rapids?"

"Are deaths from suicides deliberate or accidental?"

"Are we allowed to soak our feet in the rapids?"

"Can I throw my wife over?"

"Has anyone ever tried to go down the falls with climbing gear?"

"Do you have a barrel I can borrow?"

"Why isn't there a net under the bridge?"

"Now we know why people jump into the river. The yellow jackets make them do it."

Pointing to the American Fall, a young man wearing a devilish grin asked, "Can I go water skiing there?"

Another man politely asked, "Do you sell barrels here? My wife wants to go over the falls?"

A jolly old lady asked, "Isn't it true that visitors from Germany have to go over the falls in a keg the first time they come here?"

An old man from Austin, Texas, asked, "Where can you rent barrels for people you don't like?"

"Even the flies come to Niagara Falls to commit suicide," said a gentleman in a restaurant one morning, as he handed the waiter a glass of milk in which two flies had drowned.

Who Built the Falls?

"Once upon a time, the three rival Deities, Jupiter, Pluto, and Neptune, were each desirous of evincing their superior power in the work of creation; when Jupiter built Olympus to frighten the world with his thunder! Pluto set fire to Mount Etna! And Neptune with a dash of his Trident made the Cataract of Niagara!!"

W. A. Stephens, July, 1836

Oh, the many ways people have reacted to and described the Niagara Falls! The senses are overwhelmed. The emotions are excited. The mind tries desperately to relate to the wondrous scene. "What a wonderful thing water can become! One feels, in looking at Niagara, as if one had never seen that element before. Perhaps the most peculiar and transcendent attitude of this matchless cataract is its almost endless variety." So said the distinguished Niagarian, Peter A. Porter, in 1901. According to William H. Russell, "The falls are like one of our great statesmen. There's nothing particular about them when you first catch a view of them; but when you get close and know them better, then the power comes out, and you feel small as potatoes."

A humorous description of the falls appeared in the *Detroit Free Press* in 1884. A rural gentleman obviously tried his best to put into words his reaction to the wonder.

"Stopped Off at Niagara"

"A man, seemingly about 60 years of age, was telling people in the waiting room at the Third Street

depot yesterday that he had been East to Massachu-
setts to see his sisters, and that on the way back he
stopped off at Niagara Falls. 'That's a place I never saw,'
remarked a woman with a poke-bonnet (a bonnet with
projecting front brim) on.

'You didn't! Well, you've missed the awfullest sight
on earth! I was just stunned.'

'What is it like?' she asked.

Well, there's a river, and the falls, and lots of hotels,
and several Injuns, and the bridle veil, and lord only
knows what else. If my woman had abeen along she'd
have wilted right down.'

'There's water there, I suppose?'

'Oh, heaps of it. It pours and thunders and roars and
foams and bumps around in the terriblest manner. You
have bit on a shirtbutton in a piece of pie, haven't you?'

'No, sir.'

'Well, the feeling was about the same—kinder
shivery. Why, the biggest man that ever lived ain't half
as big as Niagara Falls! Let him stand thar and see that
'ere water tumbling over them 'ere rocks and he can't
help but feel what a miserable hoss fly he is. You've
fallen out of bed haven't you?'

'No, sir.'

'Well, it's about the same thing, you wake up and
find yourself on the floor, and you feel as if you had
been stealin' sheep or robbin' blind men.'

'What portion of the falls did you most admire?' she
asked.

'The water, mum,' he promptly replied. 'If you'd put
10,000 kegs of beer on the roof of this building and set
them all runnin' they couldn't begin with Niagara. It's
the terriblest, appallingest thing ever patented.'

'Cost you much?' inquired a gentleman.

"Bout sixty-five cents. It's pooty tight times, and
sixty-five cents don't grow on every tree, but I ain't
sorry. It's sumthin' to talk about for twenty years to
come. There's a chap in our town who used to travel
with a circus, but he'll have to take a back seat when I
git home. Flipflopping around in a circus don't begin

with Niagara Falls.'
   'So, on the whole, you were pleased, eh?'
   'Pleased! Why, I was tickled half to death! I tell you, if I had one on my farm I wouldn't sell it for no $50 in cash. I've looked into a field whar 750 fat hogs was waitn' to be sold for solid money, but it was no such sight as the falls. I've seen barns afire, and eight horses running away, and the Wabash river on a tear, but for downright appalling grandeur of the terriblest kind gim' me one look at the falls. You all orter go thar. You can't half appreciate it 'till you've gazed on the rumpus."

The Niagara Falls are beautiful throughout the four seasons, although some people prefer them in the autumn or winter. For example, when Isaac Weld visited in September 1796, he wrote, "the most favorable season for visiting the falls is about the middle of September, the time when we saw them; for then the woods are seen in all their glory, beautifully variegated with the rich tints of autumn; and the spectator is not annoyed with vermin. In the summer season you meet with rattlesnakes at every step, and mosquitoes swarm so thickly in the air, that to use a common phrase of the country, 'you might cut them with knife.' The cold nights in the beginning of September effectually banish these noxious animals."

The heights of the falls at Niagara are not constants. They have been changing since the end of the ice age, due to the lay of the land, the amount of water coming from the upper lakes, and, recently, the diversions of water to produce electrical power and supply industries and municipalities. However, since the beginning of these great diversions, the heights of the falls have not changed much more than thirty feet. Father Hennepin, "un grand menteur" (the big liar), said the falls were about 600 feet high, more than three times the true measurements. Later, in May of 1688, Baron de Lahontan said the falls were seven to eight hundred feet high.

Many years ago, people claimed to have heard the falls several miles away. In 1721, for example, a French Canadian, known only as Borassaw, said that, "The cataract makes such a prodigious noise, that people cannot hear each other speak at some miles distances; where . . . you may converse together close by it." The sound of the falls is never such that conversation cannot take place, at any distance. However, the thunder is somewhat magnified by an increase in the relative humidity or by standing downwind from the falls.

People are always taking photographs of the falls. That's expected. One day, the Falls Historian was taken aback when two ladies, one of whom was carrying a rather large tape recorder, approached him with a very unusual question. The younger lady asked,

"May I record the sound of the falls for my mother?"

People react to and describe the mist created by the falls in many ways. Some romanticize; some hypothesize; some complain. Again quoting William H. Russell, "Assuredly, this ever-rolling mighty cloud draping and over hanging the Falls adds much to their weird and wonderful beauty. Its variety of form is infinite, changing with every current of air, and altering from day to day in height and volume; but I never looked at it without fancying I could trace in the outlines the indistinct shape of a woman, with flowing hair and drooping arms, veiled in drapery—now crouching on the very surface of the flood, again towering aloft and tossing up her hands to heaven, or sinking down and bending low to the edge of the cataract, as though to drink its waters. With the aid of an active fancy, one might deem it to be the guardian spirit of the wondrous place."

According to Philip Stansbury, "The Horsehoe Fall creates a deep stunning roar, and whirls its spray volume after volume, a thousand feet into the air, till it seems to mingle with the clouds above. Fantastic shapes, giants, towers and sea-monsters, may be descried upon the spray, as it swells dark and watery upon the atmosphere. Sometimes a majestic being seems to rise, with his arms outstretched and his wings gradually expanding: his head strikes the clouds and slowly separates from the body. Now the wings and arms spread and become the boughs of a tree, waving in the wind and bending from its violence. Suddenly the mist rolls in thick folds from beneath, like the smoke of a house in flames, and mounting higher and higher assumes the form of a straight upright column, supporting the arch of the heavens. The column breaks, and as if its demolition had raised a dust from its ruins, new volumes ascend and afford new employment to the fancy."

A visitor once asked, "How do people drink that water with all that electricity in it?" A stupid question? Well, yes, or could it possibly be no? Read the following account from the August 9, 1871, *Niagara Falls Gazette*, and then decide.

"Gathering Electricity from the Mist of Niagara Falls"

"S. H. Lockett, Professor of Engineering, Louisiana University, writing to the New York *Sun*, from this place under date of the 20th says: 'While crossing the upper or new Suspension Bridge today, I had occasion, while conversing with a friend, to point toward the Falls with my walking cane. As soon as I did so, I heard distinctly at the end of my cane a buzzing noise, like that made by electricity passing from a heavily charged battery to a sharp point rod. Repeating the experiment, the same noise was heard. I stopped several passers and tried their canes with the same result, except in one case, where there was no ferrule (a metal cap or ring at the end of a cane) on the cane.

I immediately supposed this might be an electrical phenomenon and set to work to test the correctness of my supposition. I took a key and held it at arm's length toward the Falls and heard the same sound. Finally, at dark I returned to the bridge and pointed my cane in the air, and had the satisfaction of seeing a clear, beautiful electric brush on its end. The best point to observe this interesting and beautiful phenomenon is in the middle of the bridge, and the cane must be held at arm's length, so that its end may be at some distance from any part of the bridge. The success of the experiment seems to depend a good deal on the direction of the wind and the amount of vapor blown over the bridge. Today the wind is strong, and drives the mist directly from the Falls to the bridge, but an occasional shift or lulling of the wind would cause a cessation of the electrical noise or light.

My explanation of the phenomenon is this: as Franklin with his kite and key caught the lightning from the clouds of heaven, so here from the Suspension Bridge, surrounded by the vapors of the mighty Falls, we may stand and gather on our walking canes the electricity generated from the falling waters and contained in the floating mists. I think suitable arrangement might be made to collect enormous quantities of electricity from these mists, which might be used in producing grand and striking effects, thus adding another attractive feature to the sights at this wonderful place.'"

The *Gazette* did not discuss the authenticity of this article. People have often claimed to have seen the effects of static electricity by the falls. It would be hard to perform an experiment similar to Professor Lockett's from the Rainbow Bridge for two reasons: (1) it is further from the falls than the old suspension Bridge was; (2) there is much less mist now, since there is much more water diverted than in 1871.

Now for a complaint about the mist. Yes, a complaint about the mist by the falls. Ladies, please do not be offended by the following story. Sadly, the newspapers of the last century often portrayed women as nagging and complaining. Of course, such a generalization is not true for either sex. Please, do read on.

"A Woman's Idea"

"A Niagara Abuse— The Case a Prominent Lawyer Refused"

"The abuses at Niagara have a world-wide reputation and one of the awful ones was aired in a prominent lawyer's office a day or so ago.

'Is Mr. Smith (a fictitious name) in?' inquired a woman of the handsome clerk in the office referred to.

'No, he is not in at present,' was the reply.

Well I want to see him on important business; there is money in it for him.'

'You might take a chair, he will probably return soon,' said the clerk.

The anxious female sat down and patiently awaited the coming of the man she wanted to see. She had not long to tarry and soon she was telling her story to him.

'I have been down one of those inclines, said she, 'and while standing on the rocks a wave came up and wet me to the skin. What can I do about it?'

'Why, I don't see as you can do anything about it, if you mean in the way of damages.'

'That's what I mean. Here I am wet to the skin and I feel that I ought to be paid damages.'

'Well, I can only advise you that under the circumstances the best thing for you is a change of dress.'

'That's it, I haven't a change here.'

'I should suggest then that you enjoy the bright sunshine until you are dry.'

'Then you don't want the case?'

'No, thank you.'

And she left the office loudly proclaiming that because she didn't have redress with her that that was just why she felt she should have redress."

Another phenomenon by the falls, always present on sunny days, is the rainbow. Remember, to see a rainbow, the sun must be behind the observer, and the mist in front. In June of 1990, a lady asked if the rainbow by the American Fall had a name. Don't laugh. Many tourists have asked the same question. Well, way back in September of 1886, the *Niagara Falls Gazette* suggested that "the rainbow seen below the Niagara Falls be called by the name given to the steamer which carries passengers around the foot of those falls. Why? Because it is *made* of the mist."

Sometimes, Niagara's rainbows are unusual—large or multiple. Such a rare bow was described in the December 5, 1981, *Niagara Falls Gazette:*

"A Beautiful Rainbow"

"The people of Niagara are familiar with all sizes of rainbows for the pretty tokens are ever to be seen in the gorge, but those who missed seeing the one that hung suspended over the gorge at 7:45 o'clock Friday morning missed a rare treat. It was a magnificent bow. It rose from the gulf a little south of Falls Street and its line ascended very high. It was very broad and the colors were very strong and beautiful. Many stopped on the street to look at it and called others out of the stores to look at the spectacle.

One man remarked rather joyfully, 'it is not going to rain any more.' Within 15 minutes a very heavy rain was falling. The rainbows formed by Niagara's mist have not the same import attached to them as had the one that greeted Noah after his historical journey in the Ark."

What other zany things have people asked or said about the falls? Here are some offbeat inquiries:

"Where do you keep the big falls?"

"How come you have cold water going over the American Falls and hot water over the Horseshoe Falls?"

"When do they send the flaming pots over the falls, you know, the ones that illuminate it?"

"Do they keep sending the same water over and over the brink?"

"I liked it all except the roar of the water."

"It looks like a London Fog."

Written on an old post card, "Meet us at the falls when thirsty."

A young man asked, "What kind of history can there be here? The water went over a hundred years ago; it goes over today; it will go over in another hundred years."

A little boy asked, seriously, "What's behind the falls?"

"I'll bet the first Indian here said, 'Oh, my God!'" said an old lady.

"All of a sudden, the wind picked up and moved that rainbow right over there," an old woman excitedly told her guide.

An old couple asked, "How do they put the rainbow by the falls?"

"Is that smoke or steam?" a woman asked, pointing to the mist.

"One mile of walking just to see falling water," complained a little girl to her mother.

"God must have had a hard time making these falls," commented a young man.

"How did they put the lights under the falls?"

An old woman said, "I've been watching this falls disappear for the last 40 years."

"Are the falls shorter than they used to be?"

"Who built the falls?"

A man from Nevada said, "You can see the falls from Canada, but you feel them in the United States."

An old man from Italy said he knew how much water went over the falls. He and a friend stood on either side of the falls and used cups to measure the flow.

"Is there a restaurant under the falls?"

A Canadian lady said, "I was so frightened looking at the falls that my hands left impressions on the railing."

"Why is the rainbow at the bottom of the falls?"

"What time of day can you see the rainbows?"

"What was the biggest thing to go over the falls?"

"Who dyes the water green?"

*"What was the biggest thing to
go over the Falls?"*

"This atmosphere is terribly destructive to starched collars, and takes the curls out of one's whiskers with annoying celerity."

"I never experienced so much mist before. In fact, I am completely mistified."

"Why are the Falls of Niagara in sunshine like a coquette? Because they have more bows (beaux) than one."

"Grand pair of spectacles these falls are."

"Loud roars the water, o,
    Loud roars the water, o,
When I come to the falls again,
    I hope they will not spatter so."

"Here fools from all lands take of gazing their fill, in wonder that water will run down a hill."

"If I were annoyed with a nagging wife,
    Whose tongue was the bane of my every-day life,
To try to get rid of her pestilant clatter,
    I'd live on the brink of this great fall of water"

A boy asked, "What happens to the water?" "We drink it, stupid," replied his older brother.

In the spring of 1990, there appeared at the brink of the American fall a large red barrel, lying on its side. It had come down from Buffalo, having been used as a buoy for the infamous or famous, depending upon who describes it, "ice boom," a floating barrier of logs set across the Niagara River's source to control the movement of Lake Erie's ice floes into the river. The barrel, really a drum, became the subject of innumerable questions and comments from visitors, such as:

"Who put it there?"

"Is anyone in that barrel?"

"Why doesn't someone knock it over the falls?"

"Is that barrel empty?"

"Who dyes the water green?"

"Don't tell me those idiots are riding barrels over the American falls now."

"Has that barrel been over the falls?"

"Look! Someone tried to go over in a barrel and got stuck."

"Is that barrel bolted to the rocks?"

"I know who's inside that barrel," said a woman. "Jimmie Hoffa!"

Where's the Falls?

Every year, millions of people come to see Niagara Falls. Some of them stay at the local campgrounds or hostels; the rest check into the many hotels, motels, inns, or bed-and-breakfast houses. Most of this vacationing throng are delighted with their experiences at Niagara. It's understandable, however, with so many people from so many diverse cultures crowded together at such an exciting location, things do go wrong occasionally. Things, even people, get misplaced or lost. Communications are misunderstood, as are intentions. Some people just don't know what to expect. The following items illustrate some of these situations.

Overheard in a hotel lobby:

First gentleman: "I beg your pardon, but where in hell have I seen you before, sir?" Second gentleman (looking up from his newspaper): "I am sure I can't tell. What part of hell are your from, sir?"

"Did you find a contact lens?" the poor woman frantically asked everyone on Luna Island. It wasn't long before the pavement was covered with people, many on their hands and knees, searching, in vain, for the tiny piece of plastic.

After feeding a squirrel, a young woman noticed something missing. "Did anyone find a baby's pacifier?" she asked everyone nearby.

Many of the people who visit Niagara Falls wonder if "they" ever turn off the falls. Well, in modern times, such things have been done, to some degree. In 1969, for example, just the American Fall and Bridal Veil Fall were turned off for about six months by the construction of a cofferdam from the mainland to Goat Island.

Even during the last century some people were gullible enough to believe that the falls were turned off by someone on a regular basis. The following account appeared in the *Niagara Falls Gazette* on Wednesday, May 18, 1887.

"Miss Fortesque Didn't See Niagara"

"At Buffalo she learned something new about Niagara Falls. She arrived on Wednesday afternoon, and was anxious to see the cataract. Her manager was afraid some unforeseen delay might occur to prevent the lady's return in time for the evening's performance, and he said:

'It would be quite useless for you to go today. The falls are not visible on Wednesdays.'

'Indeed! And why not?'

'They always turn the water off on Wednesdays.'

'How extraordinary!' responded Miss Fortesque, and went away quite satisfied with the explanation.

Many structures have been built around the falls in the past few decades. A few of them puzzle tourists, especially the American Observation Tower and the International Water Control Dam. Pointing to one of these two structures, people often ask, "When are they going to finish that bridge?"

What probably causes most tourists problems is getting a sense of direction at Niagara. Perhaps it's because Canada is north, west, and south of the falls. This unique situation exists because of the sharp bend in the river. The border lies out in the middle of the river. The following examples show the state of confusion in which many visitors find themselves.

"Where's the falls?" asked a man standing about one thousand feet from the brink of the Horseshoe Fall.

Many people ask, "If the falls in the United States is the American Falls and the falls in Canada is the Horseshoe Falls, where is Niagara Falls?"

What Do You Do After You Do The Falls?

There are many things to do both in the vicinity and at Niagara Falls, rain or shine. Of course, if people are honeymooning, do they really care about the weather? Well, anyway, here's what some visitors have asked about Niagara's weather.

"How many inches of rainfall do you get here on clear days?"

"Where does all the wind come from?"

"How do you stop the rain for visitors?"

"What do you do in Niagara Falls on a rainy day?"

Many couples have come to Niagara Falls seeking a romantic experience. Some historians have said the custom of honeymooning became popular at Niagara because the sound of the cataracts made it difficult for amorous conversations to be overheard.

Many, many romantic words have been written by people visiting the falls. Here are some of a lighter nature.

"Do people neck in the park?"

"Where are all the honeymooners?"

Someone wrote the following poem on a postcard sent from Niagara Falls in 1904:
"Little drops of water
    Falling from on high
Separate to meet again
    Just like you and I."

"Where are all the honeymooners staying?"

A woman said she and her husband didn't honeymoon at the falls in 1969 because they heard there was no water going over the falls, and "that wouldn't be romantic."

Looking quite proud of himself, an elderly man said, "Well, I've finally brought my bride of 36 years to Niagara Falls for our honeymoon."

Wearing a great big smile, another elderly man said that he and his "lovely wife" came to Niagara Falls to celebrate their 35th wedding anniversary. When asked how they were planning to celebrate, he replied, "She's a goin' shoppin' and I'm a goin' fishin'."

Not all people who have visited the falls have felt romantic. Why, some men have said terrible things about their wives. One asked, "Can I throw my wife over?" Other men seem to be critical about the state of matrimony. One beautiful day, a wedding party assembled for a photograph session on Asenath, the First Sister Island. Among the people watching the event, and such events usually attract onlookers, was a chubby middle-aged man (not the author). Noticing that the groom didn't look any too happy, the onlooker commented, "If he's smart, he'll jump in."

Chivalry was the last thing on the mind of the man who wrote the following poem in 1837:

"I stood on the cliff, and astonished, gazed around
Saw the waters rush o'er, and heard them rebound;
And I thought if my love should slip and fall so,
She might tumble alone, for I wouldn't go."

One of the most popular habits of tourists is the tossing of coins into the rapids. Then there are some fools who enter the water to remove the coins. Both of these activities have precipitated questions such as:

"How much money has been thrown into the river?"

"Doesn't the park send anyone out to pick the money out of the holes in the water?"

"Why didn't the penny go over the falls when I threw it in the rapids?"

"Did you know there's a crazy fool in the rapids with a bag full of coins?"

People often say that the best place to view the falls is from the bottom of the gorge. Mark Twain didn't think so. "You descend a staircase . . . a hundred and fifty feet down, and stand at the edge of the water. After you have done it, you will wonder why you did it; but you will then be too late," he said.

Getting down into the gorge today is very easy, with the convenient elevators, but during the 18th century and the early part of the 19th century, descending into the gorge was sometimes very dangerous. Imagine climbing down a nearly vertical "ladder" made of vines or rope, the so-called "Indian ladder." That primitive device was the only way down and back up! Read the following story from Dow's *Anthology and Bibliography of Niagara Falls*. The incident took place in August of 1807.

"After having satisfied ourselves with the present view of these falls, and conformed to the custom of the place, by engraving our names on a rock, we proceeded to the place leading to the bottom, for which purpose I had understood there was a convenient ladder; but, upon examination, found it so old and crazy as almost to make me give over the attempt. You will perhaps excuse my timidity, when you are informed that this ladder, which is eighty feet in length, is placed in a perpendicular direction over sharp and cragged rocks; and its being spliced and bound together in several places with grapevines, did not tend to lessen the ill opinion I had already conceived respecting its sufficiency. However, there was no choice; our guide, being accustomed to the descent, had already disappeared. I endeavoured to prevail upon Mr. L. to lead the way, but to no purpose; he did not think it would pay for the trouble; and, as for his part, he had seen as much as he cared for. I was at length under the necessity of descending alone, and had already gone about half the way, when I found the poor ladder, by some accident or other, had lost four of its rounds; this circumstance, added to its constant tremulous motion, did not render my situation a whit more pleasing; so making one more effort to reach the yet distant step, and finding it impossible, without sliding down the side of the ladder, and recollecting at the same moment that I could not slide *up* again, I determined to ascend, and wait until I could provide a rope to support myself with. Having at length procured one from a neighboring house, I descended, without much difficulty, to the bottom of the ladder."

Christian Schultz

The most exciting thing to do when down in the gorge is to approach one of the cataracts as closely as possible. Early in the last century people sometimes explored behind all three of the falls, venturing only where conditions were safest. Until the early part of this century, it was customary to go on a guided tour behind the Bridal Veil Fall, the site of the famous Cave of the Winds, a natural cavernous indentation in the face of the gorge. Mark Twain wrote the following humorous account of his 1869 visit to the cave.

"Here I followed instructions, and divested myself of all my clothing, and put on a waterproof jacket and overalls. This costume is picturesque, but not beautiful. A guide, similarly dressed, led the way down a flight of winding stairs (the Biddle Stairs), which wound and wound and still kept on winding long after the thing ceased to be a novelty, and then terminated long before it had begun to be a pleasure. We were then well down under the precipice, but still considerably above the level of the river.

We now began to creep along flimsy bridges of a single plank, our persons shielded from destruction by a crazy wooden railing, to which I clung with both hands—not because I was afraid, but because I wanted to. Presently the descent became steeper, and the bridge flimsier, and sprays from the American Fall began to rain down on us in fast increasing sheets that soon became blinding, and after that our progress was mostly in the nature of groping. Now a furious wind began to rush out from behind the waterfall, which seemed determined to sweep us from the bridge, and scatter us on the rocks and among the torrents below. I remarked that I wanted to go home; but it was too late. We were almost under the monstrous wall of water thundering down from above, and speech was in vain in the midst of such a pitiless crash of sound.

In another moment the guide disappeared behind the deluge, and, bewildered by the thunder, driven helplessly by the wind and smitten by the arrowy tempest of rain, I followed. All was darkness. Such a mad storming, roaring and bellowing of warring wind and water never crazed my ears before. I bent my head, and seemed to receive the Atlantic on my back. The world seemed going to destruction. I could not see anything, the flood poured down so savagely. I raised my head, with open mouth, and the most of the American cataract went down my throat. If I had sprung a leak now I had been lost. And at this moment I discovered that the bridge had ceased, and we must trust for a foothold to the slippery and precipitous rocks."

The *Niagara Falls Gazette* Weekly of Wednesday, July 4, 1860, reported the following description of the Cave of the Winds by a correspondent of the Baltimore *Patriot.* Note the encounter with the rainbow.

"How the water dashed as we entered, how awfully the voice of God sounded in this miracle of wonders. Here was the water curtain 3 feet in depth at the edge of the cataract, widened into 5 and 20 feet by its descent and here the everlasting rock which frowned so gloomily upon the mortal, who seemed to be penetrating hidden mysteries. Never has the feeling of awe and human nothingness oppressed me as it did here. I paused almost bewildered, but the strong hand of the guide who led me with a lion's grip, conducted me out of this darkness, into the glorious light of a bow of hope which in complete circle surrounded the whole. The bow came so entirely around us that we bathed our hands in it, and it seemed as though we might heap it up . . ."

There has always been a justifiable concern about the safety of the Cave of the Winds. Today people walk in front of the Bridal Veil Fall, not behind it. They can stand on the "Hurricane Deck," a platform where the mist and wind can just about knock a person down. An elderly man was told the hurricane deck would take his breath away; he then asked, "How about gettin' it back?"

Since 1846, one or more Maid of the Mist boats have been taking people for a truly memorable ride into the great Horseshoe Fall. Every winter the boats have been moved out of the water to protect them from the ice bridges. "The Maid of the Mist has thrown off all her suitors, the gay admirers of the summer season and can afford to lay up for the winter," reported the *Niagara Falls Gazette Weekly,* in October of 1856.

The following entertaining description of a ride on a Maid boat in 1885 appeared in the August 19 *Niagara Falls Gazette.*

"'I'll (an old time hack driver is speaking) take you down and introduce you to the Captain of the Maid of the Mist. We've got to pay ten cents each to go down the inclined railroad here at the park. It's the only extra cost here. They charge that to make up the actual expense. The Maid of the Mist, that little steamer that lies at the foot of the American Falls, draws four to five foot of water. They'll charge us fifty cents each, if you want me to go along. All right. I'll go with you if you insist. These yellow oilskins here in the cabin we'll put on to keep the mist off. You see, when a man first comes to the cataract and sees this little steamer go way out to the foot of the cataract and sees her rock and pitch in the foam, he'd say those people on her are a set of fools. Three hours later, when he gets used to the place, he'll go out himself, enjoy the trip, and think there's nothing risky in it. It's the same as going down to the Cave of the Winds and under the falls. It's just like seeing Jumbo or any big thing. You want to get right near it; near enough to touch it, to look it over. People ain't satisfied until the cataract wets them all over. Sentimental young women sometimes want to jump into it.

Any danger? Well, as long as the falls go all right there is no danger. It don't make any difference how long it rains or how long there's a drought, the cataract tumbles down the same amount of water day in and day out. No big flood of water ever changes the cataract. But there is a constant wearing away of the shale rock of the bed of the cataract. We don't know what the rapids are undermining above Goat Island; we don't know what the waters under Luna Island are doing. Some day all that rocky projection may be swept away and all this risky business, as it is called, will be wiped out forever. People, however, brave sure death as if there were no danger. I well remember when the Canadian Falls yonder was of perfect horse-shoe form. Now see how the middle part is worn back. It don't look any more like a horseshoe than this steamer does. No, we're in no danger on this boat. These boatmen know what their about—know just how far to go. They wouldn't go a foot further than the safety line for all their worth. That young, dark skinned fellow in the wheel house knows his path here the same as a milkmaid knows hers to the cow pens. This machinery of the steamer is of the strongest and closely examined every day. There's about 150 feet of water under us now. Near the shore is the eddy; the water is 85 feet deep. Down yonder, under the railroad Suspension Bridge, the water is 210 feet deep. The rocky sides of the canyon go up 260 feet above the water line, but down at Lewiston they reach the high-est, 360 feet above the water line. I'll have to stop talking now; the cataract drowns out my voice.

To see Niagara a visitor should always leave this

part of the journey to the very last,' said the old driver as the oilskins were being removed after the boat had returned from the foot of the falls. 'Now anything else will be tame except the Cave of the Winds and the journey under the falls.'"

Hacked to Death

Before the Niagara Reservation was established by the State of New York in 1885, tourists were often dreadfully taken advantage of by the numerous hackmen (drivers of carriages for hire). Worse than that was the condition of the lands around the falls — covered in most places with unsightly structures. Fortunately, critics of the situation abounded. For example:

In 1856, the *Lockport Courier*, stated: "The young men of Niagara Falls have formed a Debating Club, and are to discuss the following question at their meeting: *Resolved*, that the system of Hack-driving, as carried on in our village and vicinity is a fruitful source of immorality and cheating."

According to the *Niagara Falls Gazette* of December 19, 1883, "'hacked to death' is suggested as an inscription for the tombstones of visitors who die at Niagara."

Unfortunately, there were a few critics of the formation of a natural reservation by the Falls. For example:

The May 6, 1885, *Niagara Falls Gazette* contained the following report. "Gradgrind, of the *Troy Times*, accepts the accomplished fact of the state reservation at Niagara with grumbling, threats and wry faces. It says it is a grand thing for the 'aesthetics,' 'idlers' and 'Lah-de-dah exquisites,' no doubt, but that Governor Hill will hear from the enraged tax-payers on the subject next fall."

About six months after the opening of the reservation, the following story appeared in the *Niagara Falls*

Gazette. "*Life* thinks that Niagara Park will not be completed without an array of signboards such as lend picturesqueness to the older parks of the country. *Life* suggests the following: 'Do not Tread on the Falls,' 'Do not Pluck the Islands.' And along the shore of the rapids: 'No Thoroughfare, do not Cross Here.' The Commissioners may not think these the most necessary guideboards that can be put up, but, if signs are found to be essential to the success of the park they would certainly provide them."

The following poem was written for a young lady by a famous Niagarian, Colonel Peter A. Porter, a member of the family who once owned much of the land above the falls on the American side of the river. After making a sketch in the lady's album of Father Hennepin, Robert La Salle, a Native American sachem (wise man), and a horse, with the falls in the background, the Colonel felt it necessary to include the poem. He humorously addressed what were really many serious changes that had taken place by the falls since the arrival of the Europeans. After reading the poem, the reader may want to ask if the waters still "fall as once they fell two hundred years ago."

> "An artist, underneath his sign
>   (A masterpiece, of course)
> Had written, to prevent mistakes,
>   'This represents a horse;'
> So ere I send my Album Sketch,
>   Lest connoisseurs should err,
> I think it well my Pen should be
>   My Art's interpreter.
>
> A chieftain of the Iroquois,
>   Clad in a bison's skin,
> Had led two travelers through the wood,
>   La Salle and Hennepin.
> He points, and there they, standing,
>   Gaze upon the ceaseless flow

Of waters falling as they fell
    Two hundred years ago.

Those three are gone,
    And little heed our worldly gain or loss
The Chief, the Soldier of the Sword,
    The Soldier of the Cross.
One died in battle, one in bed,
    And one by secret foe;
But the waters fall as once they fell
    Two hundred years ago.

Ah, me! What myriads of men, since then,
    Have come and gone;
What states have risen and decayed,
    What prizes lost or won;
What varied tricks the juggler, Time,
    Has played with all below;
But the waters fall as once they fell
    Two hundred years ago.

What troops of tourists have encamped
    Upon the river's brink;
What poets shed their countless quills,
    Niagaras of ink;
What artist armies tried to fix
    The evanescent bow
Of waters falling as they fell
    Two hundred years ago.

And stately inns feed scores of guests
    From well replenished larder,
And hackmen drive their horses hard,
    But drive a bargain harder;
And screaming locomotives
    Rush to and fro
And the waters fall as once they fell
    Two hundred years ago.

And brides of every age and clime
　　Frequent the island's bower,
And gaze from off the stone-built porch—
　　Hence called the Bridal Tower—
And many a lunar belle goes forth
　　To meet Lunar beau,
By the waters falling as they fell
　　Two hundred years ago.

And bridges bind thy breast, O stream!
　　And buzzing millwheels turn,
To shoe, like Samson, thou art forced
　　Thy daily bread to earn;
And steamers splash thy milk-white waves,
　　Exulting as they go,
But the waters fall as once they fell
　　Two hundred years ago.

Thy banks no longer are the same
　　That early travelers found them,
But break and crumble now and then
　　Like other banks around them;
And on the verge our life sweeps on—
　　Alternate joy and woe,
But the waters fall as once they fell
　　Two hundred years ago.

Thus phantoms of a by-gone age
　　Have melted like the spray;
And in our turn we too shall pass,
　　The phantoms of today:
But the armies of the coming time
　　Shall watch the ceaseless flow
Of waters falling as they fell
　　Two hundred years ago."

"What time do they turn the water off?" That is a common
question asked by tourists, especially since the 1950's, when
50 to 75 percent of the upper Niagara River began to be
diverted to the large new power stations. The control of the

water has been debated for many years. The following poem, written by Wallace Irwin in 1905, deals with the diversion of Niagara's waters.

"Niagara Be Dammed"

'Them beauties o' Nature,' said Senator Grabb,
As he spat on the floor of Justitia's halls,
'Is pretty enough and artistic enough—
Referrin', of course, to Niagara Falls,
Whose waters go rumblin' and mumblin' and grumblin'
And tearin' and stumblin' and bumblin' and tumblin'
And foamin' and roarin' and plungin' and pourin'
And wastin' the waters God gave to us creechers
To wash down our liquor and washup up our feechers—
Then what in the deuce
Is the swish-bingled use
O'keepin' them noisy old cataracts busy
To give folks a headache and make people dizzy?

'Some poets and children and cripples and fools
They say that them Falls is eternal.
That so?
Say, what is Eternity, Nature, and God
Compared to the Inter-Graft Gaslighting Co.?
Could all the durn waterfalls born in creation
Compete with a sugar or soap corporation?
But Nature, you feel,
Has a voice in the deal?
She ain't For I'm deaf both in that ear and this un—
If Nature talks Money I'm willin' to listen!'"

Most of the poeple who visit Niagara Falls and walk through the beautiful parks on both sides of the river show respect for the environment. Unfortunately, some visitors think nothing of littering either the land or the water. In an effort to embarass the litterbugs on Goat Island, the following satirical essay was composed a few years ago. There does now seem to be less litter on the island.

"Startling New Plants Discovered on Goat Island"

"Many world-famous naturalists and botanists have visited Goat Island since the 18th century, and they have been quite impressed by its native flora. Over nine hundred different species of plants were cataloged about one century ago, a notable but poorly disseminated fact. Upon that temperate Eden there once grew a diversity of plants unlike that in any other place in North America of similar acreage. Unfortunately, human activities have diminished that diversity, i.e. until the past few decades.

Since the 1960's, there has been a startling introduction of strange and entirely new forms of plant life on Goat Island. Spreading over the island's shores and paths, the newcomers have become very noticeable. There seems to be a definite connection between humans and the proliferation of the new plants.

Most of the new plants have been classified scientifically. The most common phylum or group is Paperum. Its members live a fairly long time, but they do eventually fade and decay. The Papera flourishing on Goat Island are called Sheeta, Plata, Strawnia, Newsia, Diapera, and Kleenyxa. Paperae Sheetae, the most abundant members of this phylum, resemble tumbleweed because of their habit of blowing around in the wind.

The next most abundant phylum is Plasticius, represented by the species Sheetius, Cupsius, Forka, Spoonum, Strawanius, and Lida. These plants are apparently capable of living for thousands of years.

Another phylum thriving on the island is Cigaretta, represented by the two species Filtera and Butta. These plants are quite hardy, allowing them to even grow on asphalt or concrete. They also like growing around benches.

Popsius and Beerius are the two most common members of the phylum Glassium. They are scattered all over the island, often breaking apart into smaller pieces, undoubtedly some form of asexual production.

The last new phylum is called Alumina, and it is represented by Foilium and Canius. Canius has actually become somewhat endangered in recent years, because some humans find it to be of value. Before people were picking windflowers, causing some species to disappear from the island. Will a similar fate befall poor Canius?

Except for Canius, the new plants on Goat Island seem to have a bright future, despite the efforts of state workers to remove or control them. This effort has met with some success, but as more and more people visit the island, more of the plants appear just about everywhere, even inside the metal cylinders called "waste receptacles." Along just about every path, there is a Cupsius here, Sheeta there. Who knows? In time, the island may be covered with Sheetae!"

Paul Gromosiak

Can You Tell Me
Me What I Don't Know?

Many times tourists preface a question with, "You've probably been asked this a million times before, but...," or, "this is a stupid question, but...." All people who work in the parks by the falls serving the public must endure these and other repetitious questions, but they usually provide the answers with a smile. Wouldn't it be nice, however, to make answering questions a lot easier? The following article from the *Niagara Falls Gazette* of August 8, 1891, suggests a method to do just that.

"Jack McCloy's Idea"

"The number of questions that are put to Jack McCloy at the inclined railway in Prospect Park each day is astonishing. Every one of them is answered good naturedly, and the many hundreds of people who visit Niagara have reason to know that Jack McCloy is the right man in the right place. Jack is quite a mechanic and makes all the needed repairs about the cars and machinery of the railway. He is a deep thinker, too, and has many good ideas. One that struck him the other day must be classed as remarkably bright and is destined to add to the charm of a visit to Niagara. Perhaps the city folk will not be so delighted with it as will the people from the small towns in Canada and the states. To this latter class it will form a wonderful attraction and reveal to them, probably for the first time, the great depth of invention men like Edison are capable of.

McCloy's idea is to get a phonograph and have the cylinder loaded so that something about like this will be heard at all points within the building: 'Ten cents — Down and up — Right away, get in — You can walk down for nothing—Ten cents pays for both ways — Get in the car if you are going down — The stairs are free — The car starts right off — There is no danger — If the boat is at the dock it will leave right away — You get your tickets at the foot of the incline for the boat — three in a seat there — One dime — Yes, it is good to come up, it says so on the back — No, give it to the man down stairs when you come up — Get in the car there — Ten cents — Hurry up — Take the next car on the other side — There are 251 stairs — The distance down is 320 feet — Perpendicular is 170 feet —The angle is 30 degrees — We never had an accident — I have been here nine years — The Park was made free in '85 — Ten cents pays for both ways — No charge for the little one — Take that seat — Mr. Athearn is in the office —It is 3:30 — No, I don't know what time the train leaves —Ten cents — We stop running soon after 6 o'clock — It takes the boat about 25 minutes — How many? — That's an electric bell — One ring is to start, three for the boat to wait — Yes, it is handy — Hot, well I should say so —Ten cents — Yes, both ways, if you are going get in the car — It is operated by water power — Mr. Welch! I guess he went over on the Island

— If I didn't move the lever over the car would continue right along up when I started it — Buy your tickets here — No, that ticket is no good — All aboard — You can walk down and ride up; it will cost you five cents — thanks, I will smoke it after supper — You will find ice water just outside that door — Ten cents — No, we don't sell postal cards — No stamps — McMullen is down on the point — All aboard.'"

The author of this book has worked as a volunteer for the Schoellkopf Geological Museum in the Niagara Reservation, as a falls historian. Since 1984, he has been answering questions from tens of thousands of visitors. Once and awhile, he is asked zany questions, or he hears crazy comments. Here are a few.

"Can you tell me what I don't know?"

"Can I throw my kids over (the falls)?"

"Are there any birds in Toronto, other than gulls?"

"What was the song whistled to Marilyn Monroe in the movie, *Niagara?*" ("Kiss")

On Monday, July 14, 1986, a man who looked about 70 years old said he used to visit the falls from Buffalo before there as a park. Since park opened in 1885, that would make the man over 100 years old.

A bearded young man slowly rode his bicycle on Goat Island, muttering to himself over and over, "it's going to be dark tonight."

Two very happy young men from Australia arrived on Luna Island, clapped their hands quickly, and shouted to the large crowd, "hi, friends!"

A mother to her restless and thirsty child, "if I throw you in, you can get a drink, but I might never see you again."

A little boy asked, "is all the "U" Falls in the US?"

"The Great Lakes are the OPEC of fresh water," a young man said.

About the Author

Thousands of visitors from around the world have enjoyed reading Paul Gromosiak's first two books on Niagara Falls. *Soaring Gulls and Bowing Trees: The History of the Islands Above Niagara Falls* and *Answers to the 100 Most Common Questions About Niagara Falls* offered scores of historical insights into one of the world's most visited attractions. The latter book is in its fourth printing.

In his new book, *Zany Niagara: The Funny Things People Say About Niagara Falls*, Gromosiak treats readers to an offbeat armchair tour.

A former chemist and science and mathematics teacher in the Niagara Falls, New York school system, Gromosiak has studied local history all of his adult life. He has generously shared his knowledge with visitors and local people since 1984, as a volunteer local historian at the Niagara Reservation.

Gromosiak is also a popular guest on the local speaking circuit. He has shared his fascinating, humor-laden insights with dozens of groups.

Western New York Wares, Inc.

Zany Niagara: The Funny Things People Say About Niagara Falls — An offbeat armchair tour of one of the the world's most visited attractions. **$4.95**

Rescue of a Landmark: Frank Lloyd Wright's Darwin D. Martin House — Filled with beautiful color and black-and-white photographs, this book by art historian Marjorie L. Quinlan explores the rich history and subsequent rescue of a noted landmark. **$9.95**

Quotable Cuomo: The Mario Years — Hundreds of lively quotes from one of America's most effective public speakers are included in this book. Compiled by Brian Meyer and Mary Murray, the book contains more than a dozen photographs of Mario Cuomo and includes a comprehensive index. The consummate quote book for Cuomo fans and foes. **$5.95**

Hometown Heroes: Western New Yorkers in Desert Storm — More than one hundred people were interviewed, their experiences woven together in an enlightening text that affords a unique glimpse of Desert Storm. Written by Brian Meyer and Tom Connolly, this is not a book about war. Rather, it's a book about people and how their lives were touched by Desert Storm. **$5.95**

Designated Landmarks of the Niagara Frontier — About 100 landmarks spring to life in a fascinating look at the region's architectural past. Written by Austin Fox and illustrated by Lawrence McIntyre. **$13.95**

Symbol & Show: The Pan-American Exposition of 1901 — Written by Austin Fox and illustrated by Lawrence McIntyre, this book showcases one of Buffalo's most significant events. **$13.95**

Answers to the 100 Most Common Questions About Niagara Falls — Volunteer local falls historian Paul Gromosiak spent four summers at Niagara Falls, chatting with 40,000 tourists. This invaluable guide answers the most commonly asked questions. **$3.50**

Soaring Gulls and Bowing Trees: The History of the Islands Above Niagara Falls — Color photographs and insightful text focus on the magnetism and history of Niagara Falls. **$9.95**

Buffalo: A Bull's Eye View — Bizarre tales and quotes offer a humorous look at Western New York. This offbeat almanac contains 600 anecdotes and illustrations. **$4.95**

The Cheap Gourmets' Dining Guide to the Niagara Frontier (Now in its third edition!) — Doug and Polly Smith visit more than 50 restaurants. The eateries are categorized as "Very Cheap," "Pretty Cheap" and "Not Cheap at All." **$5.95**

Buffalo Bluff — A game of cunning hometown deception where players try to trick opponents by creating lies about local people, places and events. **$13.95**

Buffalo Chips (The Book) — Popular local cartoonist Tom Stratton has penned more than 100 humorous cartoons and essays in this 144-page book. **$6.95**

(See order form on next page)

Sing a Song of Six Packs — Buffalo politics is set to music in hilarious song parodies that focus on the feisty reign of Mayor Jimmy Griffin. Cassette tape and illustrated book. **$11.95**

Western New York Trivia Quotient—Crammed with 1,300 questions about the region. Fun and educational. **$7.95**

Buffalo's Waterfront: A Guidebook — Filled with drawings and maps, this fascinating armchair tour of the region's shoreline was edited by Tim Tielman and published by the Preservation Coalition of Erie County. More than 100 waterfront sites are showcased. **$5.95**

Please include 8% sales tax and $1 for shipping/handling costs. Send orders to:

> **Western New York Wares Inc.**
> **P.O. Box 733**
> **Ellicott Station**
> **Buffalo, New York 14205**

About the Publisher

Western New York's most innovative publishing company sprouted its roots in trivial turf.

The year was 1984. The trivia craze was taking the nation by storm. Some friends sat in a North Buffalo living room playing one of the more popular games. Brian Meyer casually remarked that someone should concoct a trivia game that focused on Buffalo-area people, places and events.

Several months later, *Western New York Trivia Quotient* was born. The game sold out its first edition in seven weeks, catapulting it into a second edition.

A year later, Meyer decided to compile a book of quotations that chronicled the unpredictable utterings of Buffalo's feisty mayor. *The World According to Griffin* was a popular stocking-stuffer during the 1985 holiday season.

Meyer has co-authored many other books, including *Buffalo: A Bull's Eye View, Quotable Cuomo: The Mario Years* and *Hometown Heroes: Western New Yorkers in Desert Storm.* The *Buffalo News* has called Meyer one of the region's "most prolific authors."

Meyer Enterprises became a corporation in 1989. Western New York Wares Inc. has published the works of more than a dozen local authors. Among the more popular titles: *The Cheap Gourmets' Dining Guide to the Niagara Frontier* and *Niagara Falls Q & A: Answers to the 100 Most Common Questions about Niagara Falls.*

During its first seven years in existence, the company has sold nearly 40,000 copies of its Buffalo-oriented books and games.

Meyer is managing editor of news at WBEN Radio, where he has worked since 1982. The Buffalo native graduated from St. Joseph's Collegiate Institute and from Marquette University.

Western New York Wares Inc. has plans to publish no fewer than 15 new titles over the next five years.

Appendix

You might want to record, on these blank pages, zany comments or questions you, your companions, or strangers said at Niagara Falls. Come on! you must have heard or said something worth remembering.